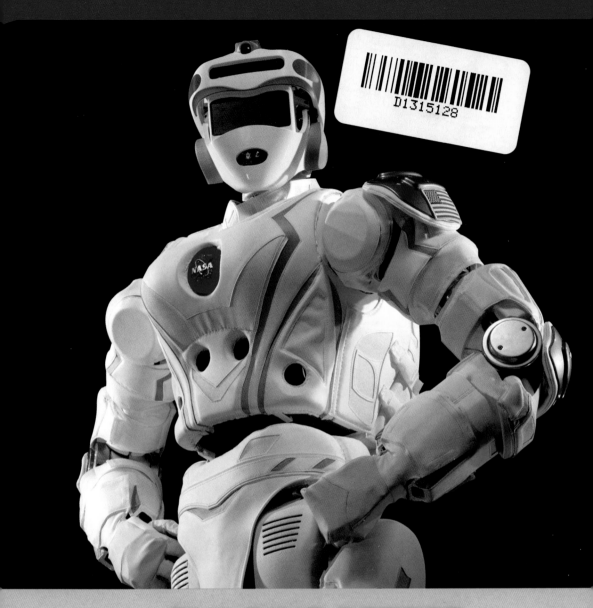

BUILDING BETTER
ROBOTS

by Angie Smibert

www.12StoryLibrary.com

12-Story Library is an imprint of Peterson Publishing Company and Press Room Editions.

Produced for 12-Story Library by Red Line Editorial

Photographs ©: NASA, cover, 1, 12, 13, 14, 15; Guilhem Vellut CC2.0, 4; wi6995/ Shutterstock Images, 5; Staff Sgt. Bernardo Fuller, 6; Saginaw Future Inc. CC2.0, 7; RIC CC2.0, 8; Veterans Affairs and DEKA CC2.0, 9; Stefan Rousseau/PA Wire URN:13476933/ AP Images, 10; Steve Jurvetson CC2.0, 11; Kyle J. O. Olson/USMC, 16; Koichi Nakamura/ The Yomiuri Shimbun/AP Images, 17; Steve Lodefink CC2.0, 18; Gwoeii/Shutterstock Images, 19, 28; US Air Force, 20; Andri Koolme CC2.0, 21; John F. Williams/US Navy, 22, 23, 29; Maurizio Pesce CC 2.0, 24, 25; Dick Thomas Johnson CC2.0, 26, 27

Library of Congress Cataloging-in-Publication Data
Cataloging-in-publication information is on file with the Library of Congress.
978-1-63235-374-0 (hardcover)
978-1-63235-391-7 (paperback)
978-1-62143-515-0 (hosted ebook)

Printed in the United States of America
Mankato, MN
May, 2016

Access free, up-to-date content on this topic plus a full digital version of this book. Scan the QR code on page 31 or use your school's login at 12StoryLibrary.com.

Table of Contents

Humans Have Long Dreamed of Creating Robots

Humans have built devices that move or act like people and animals for hundreds of years. In the 1700s, inventors built automata, or mechanical puppets. Automata could move their arms, lips, or other body parts. Some could write. Some could draw. One famous automaton could play 12 songs on a flute. But none of these machines could learn new tasks. Each device was built to do one thing. They were not true robots.

The first robot was invented in the 1950s. Unimate was an industrial robot. It was installed at General Motors in 1961. Unimate had a long arm that stacked hot pieces of metal. The robot followed instructions programmed into its control system. It used the instructions to make decisions about its job. And that is perhaps the

Many automata were designed to look and act like humans.

2.3 million

Estimated number of industrial robots in the world by the end of 2018.

- People have been trying to build robots for centuries.
- Unimate, the first modern robot, was created in the 1950s.
- Robots are programmable machines that can make decisions.
- Interacting with the world is still a challenge for robots.

Industrial robots work well for simple, repetitive tasks.

most basic definition of a robot. Robots are programmable machines that can interact with the world around them.

Sensors feed robots with images, sounds, and other information about their surroundings. Control systems tell robots how to react. Many robots can handle objects using devices at the ends of their arms. These devices are called end effectors. Some robots are mobile. There are robots that walk, roll on wheels, or do both.

Until recently, robots tended to do one thing each. Some welded cars. Others vacuumed floors. They were able to do these things as long as they were in fixed settings.

The world is an unpredictable place for robots. It's full of obstacles, uneven ground, and people. Today's robot makers are creating machines that are more adaptable. Builders hope to make robots that can more easily navigate outside the lab, travel where we can't go, and even socialize with people.

5

Da Vinci Provides a Steady Hand

The Da Vinci robot's four arms hover over a patient. It is performing surgery. Each of the robot's arms twitches only slightly as it operates. The robot has tiny tools and a 3-D camera at the end of one of its arms. The arms have been inserted through small slits in the patient's skin. The tools slice and burn away a tumor on her kidney. There's very little blood. The patient will recover from surgery quickly.

Da Vinci is not doing all of this on its own, though. A surgeon controls Da Vinci through a console in the corner of the operating room. The surgeon can see inside the patient using the robot's 3-D camera system. She uses the hand controllers to move the scalpel and laser tools. Da Vinci smooths out the doctor's motions, including shaky hand movements. The robot makes it possible for surgeons to be very precise. But the doctor makes the medical decisions.

Other surgical robots today take the human further out of the picture. Humans do not control every movement with some robots.

The Da Vinci robot helps give surgeons steady hands.

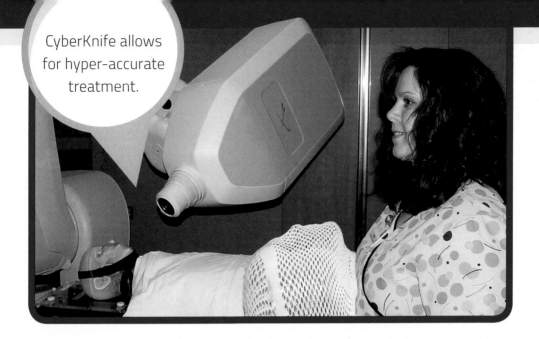

CyberKnife allows for hyper-accurate treatment.

For example, a robot called CyberKnife targets cancer cells with radiation on its own. It adjusts if the patient moves. Since this robot is so accurate, therapy can sometimes be completed in just one week.

Traditional treatment affects a much larger area of patients' bodies over a longer period of time.

SURGICAL SNAKEBOT

Carnegie Mellon University is developing a surgical robot shaped like a snake. The robot is called Flex. It is designed to fit into curving areas of the body such as the throat, nose, ears, or heart valves. Flex has a camera and lights at its end. Small surgical tools can be threaded through Flex's body. A doctor can operate the snakebot using a joystick.

400,000

Approximate number of surgeries done by Da Vinci robots per year.

- Surgeons can operate using robots.
- Da Vinci has four arms with tiny tools and a camera.
- A human operates the robot through a console.
- The robot smooths out the surgeon's motions.
- Other surgical robots today can operate with less human control.

Bionic Limbs Help People Move Naturally Again

A man steps across his hospital room. His new right leg moves forward without a stumble. He does not need to think about it. The leg does the thinking for him. The patient is wearing an Össur Symbionic Leg. It was the first bionic leg available for people to buy. The limb is artificial. But it can interact with the human body. Sensors in the limb read the person's movements. They also scan the outside world. The leg interprets the information. It figures out the best angle to swing the foot forward at. The leg even has a stumble-recovery mode that helps prevent falls.

Designing a bionic arm is more difficult than coming up with a bionic leg. The wearer must be able to move the shoulder, elbow, and wrist joints. He or she also needs fingers that flex and hold objects. The DEKA arm is the first commercially

Bionic legs allow amputees to do everyday activities such as climbing stairs.

The DEKA arm is capable of handling delicate objects.

available arm capable of doing these movements at the same time. The arm's sensors pick up electrical signals from the person's muscles. The DEKA arm then turns these signals into movements. The wearer can control multiple joints and use individual fingers. Sensors even send feedback to the wearer. The person can tell how firmly he or she is gripping something, for example. This robotic arm allows the person to handle an egg or even unlock a door.

185,000
Average number of people who lose limbs per year in the United States.

- Researchers use robotics to replace limbs.
- Bionic limbs interact with a person's natural functions.
- Limbs use sensors to help the wearer move more naturally.
- It is more difficult to design a bionic arm than to design a bionic leg.

9

Robot Helps Paralyzed Woman Complete Marathon

In 2007, Claire Lomas became paralyzed from the chest down in an accident. In 2012, she crossed the finish line of a marathon. It took her longer than the other runners, but she finished. She was wearing a robotic exoskeleton called the ReWalk. An exoskeleton is a wearable robot. It fits over the torso, legs, and feet. This robot reads small shifts in balance, such as a forward tilt, to tell it what to do. Motors power the hip and knee joints.

Lomas's ReWalk was the first one approved for home use. Other

Hundreds cheer on Claire Lomas as she nears the finish line of the London Marathon.

Exoskeletons can also help able-bodied people carry heavy loads with less stress on their bodies.

EXOSKELETONS IN SPACE

Researchers are creating exoskeletons that can control robots remotely. A human operator would wear an exoskeleton. The robot would then act out the operator's movements. The technology would be especially helpful in space and other dangerous environments. The European Space Agency is creating an exoskeleton to operate a robot outside of the International Space Station or on Mars.

Exoskeletons can also help able-bodied people carry heavy loads with less stress on their bodies.

exoskeletons, such as the Ekso, are designed for therapy. The Ekso helps people recover from spinal cord, nerve, or brain injuries. These patients work with physical therapists. The patients use the Ekso to relearn how to walk. When used for this purpose, they must try to walk. The Ekso supports and assists their efforts. As a patient grows stronger, the Ekso is smart enough to give the patient less and less help.

16
Number of days it took Lomas to complete the marathon.

- Lomas's exoskeleton was the first such robot to be approved for home use.
- An exoskeleton is a wearable robot.
- It picks up slight movements and helps move the rest of the body.
- Robots can also be used to help people learn to walk again.

R2 Takes a Giant Leap for Robo-kind

In 2011, a robot joined the crew of the International Space Station (ISS). Robonaut 2, or R2, is a humanoid robot. It is designed to handle the same tools as astronauts. Astronauts and ground crew control R2 with a laptop. R2 can take over some of the repetitive and dangerous jobs on the ISS and beyond. As technology gets better, R2 will free up the rest of the crew for other work. The robot's torso attaches to workbenches and other equipment. On a Mars mission, R2 could be attached to a rover, creating a humanoid robot with a rover lower half.

R2 can perform work alongside humans in the International Space Station.

4
Number of Robonauts in existence.

- Robonaut 2 is a humanoid robot.
- It joined the crew of the ISS in 2011.
- R2 can do many of the same tasks the astronauts do.
- R2 got climbing legs in 2014.
- The legs help the robot climb and anchor on the ISS.

The R5 Valkyrie represents the next generation of space robots.

GETTING READY FOR MARS

While R2 was being tested on the ISS, the National Aeronautics and Space Administration (NASA) built a new robot, the R5 Valkyrie. Unlike R2, Valkyrie is designed to work on planets with gravity. R5 is also more able to reason for itself. In 2015, NASA gave R5 robots to two universities with a new challenge: get Valkyrie ready for Mars. The two schools are finding ways to prepare the R5 for the red planet.

In 2014, R2's climbing legs arrived on the ISS. The legs give the robot more mobility in space, where there is little gravity. The legs have seven joints. Instead of feet, each leg has an end effector. These allow the legs to hook onto handrails in and around the ISS. R2 can climb and anchor itself using its legs. This frees up both hands for helping astronauts.

Rovers Go Where No Person Has Gone Before

Most of our exploration of the universe has been done using robots. We've sent orbiters, landers, and probes to planets, moons, and asteroids. Two probes have even left the solar system. The most advanced robot explorers are the Mars rovers. In 2012, NASA's *Curiosity* rover landed on Mars. The rover is approximately the size of a car. It carries its own lab. *Curiosity*'s mission is to explore the Gale Crater, which is 96 miles (154 km) wide. The robot runs tests on soil. It's looking for the building

Robotic arms help lift and move large objects in space.

140 million

Average distance, in miles (225 million km), from Earth to Mars.

- NASA has been exploring space with robots for many years.
- *Curiosity* began exploring Mars in 2012.
- The rover's mission is to find signs of life.
- *Curiosity* has its own lab that can test rock and soil.
- The rover found that Mars could have once supported life.

ASTEROID MINING

Robots may soon be exploring and mining asteroids. Several companies have plans to launch robotic miners. The robots would mine asteroids for water and minerals. These could be brought back to Earth. They could also be used for buildings and supplies for human explorers in space.

blocks of life, including water and organic compounds. The rover carries a 10-instrument package of tools and sensors. With its seven-foot (2-m) arm, *Curiosity* can scoop up samples. Inside, the rover vaporizes the samples. It tests the gases, and determines the chemicals in the sample. *Curiosity* also has a tool for detecting underground ice. The instrument shoots a beam of neutrons into the ground. Water takes in more neutrons than soil does. So if the beam hits ice, *Curiosity* can detect it. In early 2013, *Curiosity* found

Curiosity is a roving laboratory on Mars.

that the Gale Crater could have supported early stages of life at one time. Later that same year, the rover found evidence of water in martian soil. *Curiosity* was still going in 2016. Another mission was scheduled to use a rover similar to *Curiosity* in 2020.

15

Nature Inspires Roboticists

Robot designers often turn to nature for inspiration. A robot named Big Dog mimics how real dogs move. The four-footed robot can run. It can scramble up hills as sure-footedly as a real dog. Big Dog was made to accompany soldiers in the battlefield. It can carry equipment on its back. Even a kick won't topple the robot over. Big Dog can adjust its footing to stay upright. The same company that makes Big Dog also makes Cheetah. Cheetah copies the stride of a real cheetah. It can run faster than the fastest human. Basing robots on nature helps scientists design efficient movements in machines.

Other scientists are working on robots that move or act like snakes, plant roots, flying insects, crabs, and

The US military designs mobile robots to help carry equipment.

Swimming snake-like robots may also be used for search and rescue.

many other things. Researchers at Virginia Tech are making a robot jellyfish for the US Navy. It will be used for surveillance during search-and-rescue operations. Jellyfish move through the water by contracting their bells. The umbrella-like bells push out water. This pushes the jellyfish forward. Metal and plastics cannot flex as gracefully as jellyfish, though. Scientists instead used shape-memory metal alloys to copy the jellyfish's action. These smart metals can bend and return to their original shape. Another smart material creates heat when it touches the hydrogen and oxygen in the water. The jellyfish robot uses the heat to power itself.

29
Speed, in miles per hour (47 km/h), of the Cheetah robot.

- Scientists often study nature in order to design robots.
- Robots imitate animals, insects, and even plants.
- Some robots copy animal movements, such as walking or swimming.
- Creating robots based on nature often leads to new discoveries.

Robot Swarm Uses Teamwork to Do Big Things

In nature, some types of insects, such as bees, swarm together. Each member of the swarm follows the others. The insects spread out just far enough not to run into each other. They move as a single unit around objects. Insects do this by instinct. A swarm of bees can move to a new hive as an entire colony.

Scientists have taken insects' swarming abilities to new levels. In 2012, the University of Pennsylvania's robotics lab made flying robots that could also swarm. The robots are small quadcopters. A quadcopter is like a helicopter. But it has four rotors instead of one. Each robot obeys simple rules. Like bees, they can fly in formation. Sensors

Quadcopters are one type of swarming robot.

Swarming robots can work together to perform larger tasks.

tell the robots where they are and how close they are to objects. People can send the swarm signals to move in certain formations or to pick up objects. The swarm is more effective than any one of the robots alone. They work together to do big things. For example, a swarm with cameras can search buildings during a disaster. Other applications range from exploring Mars to building homes. For instance, a swarm of robots might easily move construction materials or even lay bricks.

1,024
Number of robots in the largest swarm to date.

- Swarming insects have inspired a new field of robotics.
- Insects such as bees can act together as a swarm.
- Each member of a robot swarm follows simple rules.
- Together, the swarm can do larger tasks.

THINK ABOUT IT

Based on what you read on these pages, explain how robots work together like insects.

Drones Take to the Skies

Aircraft without pilots may soon become a common sight. The military has been making unmanned aerial vehicles (UAVs), or drones, for many years. But it wasn't until computer advances in the 1980s and 1990s that modern drones emerged. The US military has drones with cameras and weapons. It uses them on the battlefield.

Now, drones are also being used for surveying, filmmaking, search and rescue, law enforcement, and agriculture. Both Google and Amazon plan to deliver packages with drones. And everyday people can now buy their own drones.

Drones fall into two categories: remotely piloted and

Military drones help keep pilots out of harm's way.

400

Maximum height, in feet (122 m), a personal drone is allowed to fly in the United States.

- Drones are unmanned aircraft.
- The military has been making drones for decades.
- Drones can fly on their own or be controlled remotely.
- Consumers can buy drones in the United States.
- Rules limit where and how people use their drones.

autonomous. Autonomous means the aircraft can steer without human control. Most drones available in the stores are remotely piloted. Some have built-in automated functions, such as automatic return. Drones may also have global positioning systems, cameras, and sensors that help them avoid collisions. But most drones people can buy are not strictly robotic. The user controls most of the drone's movements. Some industrial drones allow the user to program flight paths, heights, and speeds. But the US Federal Aviation Administration requires operators to keep drones within sight.

Drones for personal use are remote controlled.

THINK ABOUT IT

Some people are worried drones might cause issues in air safety and privacy. Research this topic. What are some concerns people have?

HUBO Wins Robotics Challenge

"Ladies and gentlemen, start your robots," the announcer yelled. It was the finals of the DARPA Robotics Challenge (DRC), held in June 2015. One by one, the robots attempted to complete an obstacle course in the fastest time. When it was HUBO's turn, the robot quickly drove an all-terrain vehicle around the obstacles in the first leg of the course. HUBO is a South Korean–made humanoid robot. Next came the tricky part. HUBO pulled itself out of the car. It walked to the next obstacle: a closed door. The robot twisted the doorknob with its hand and walked through to the other challenges.

44:28
Time, in minutes and seconds, it took HUBO to complete the final DRC course.

- HUBO won the first DARPA Robotics Challenge.
- The DRC was held in order to advance humanoid robot research.
- The DRC final was an obstacle course.
- Robots had to complete eight tasks in under an hour.
- The top three teams won money to continue their research.

A humanoid robot exits an all-terrain vehicle during the DRC.

HUBO uses a tool to cut through a wall during the DRC.

THINK ABOUT IT

Why did the organizers start the DARPA Robotics Challenge? Use the information on these pages to form your answer.

Before the course was done, HUBO had used a power tool to cut a hole in a wall, flipped circuit breakers, turned an industrial valve, and walked over rubble. The final task was for the robot to walk up a flight of stairs. These obstacles may seem simple. But they are difficult for robots, especially with limited human control. The robots must figure out how to get past most of the obstacles based on their programming. They have one hour to complete the course. HUBO won the competition. It finished the course in less than 45 minutes.

The DRC was started after the Fukushima nuclear accident in Japan in March 2011. The disaster made many scientists realize robots that could go into dangerous areas were important. This meant the robots needed to be able to do the things human rescuers could do: travel over rough terrain, open doors, use tools, navigate stairs, and even make decisions without guidance. The goal of the DRC was to push research forward in these areas.

Over the course of years, robot teams from universities and robotics companies competed in a series of DRC competitions. In the finals, 23 teams competed. The top three finishers won a total of $3.5 million to continue their research.

Modular Robots Shape-Shift

In the movies, robots can change themselves into cars or other forms. Real robots can't quite do that yet. But scientists are designing modular robots. These robots can arrange and possibly even assemble themselves. They can change their shape to fit what they need to do. And they can take on many shapes by switching around their modules.

Modules are small, simple robotic pieces. They can be combined in different ways. Several research groups are creating modular robots. For example, people at the Massachusetts Institute of Technology designed cube-shaped modules called M-Blocks. The blocks snap together with magnets. People use signals to direct how the cubes

Different modular blocks perform different functions.

6

Number of connections each Cubelet can make with another.

- Modular robots are made up of small, simple pieces.
- They can be arranged to form many different robots.
- In the future, some may be able to assemble themselves according to the task.

THINK ABOUT IT

Do a little outside research. What are some interesting uses for modular robots?

are arranged. In the future, researchers hope to make cubes that can arrange themselves according to the task.

A few modular robotics kits are sold as

educational toys. For example, Cubelets are blocks used for building robots. Different Cubelet blocks perform different functions, such as sensing or moving. The user can put the blocks together to form thousands of different robots.

> Cubelets can be used to make robotic toys.

25

Social Robot Cracks Jokes

To live and work with humans, robots need to understand and act like humans. Understanding humans often involves being able to read facial expressions, gestures, body language, and tone of voice. Several scientists have made great progress in this area.

A few social robots are already at work. In June 2014, a robot called Pepper began greeting customers at Softbank Mobile stores in Japan. Pepper is designed to interact with humans. Its makers say Pepper can make small talk, recognize and react to emotions, and move on its own. Pepper uses cameras and sensors to move around safely. The robot uses other sensors to analyze customers' voices, facial expressions, and body movements. Pepper changes

Pepper can gauge how people are feeling and react accordingly.

More than anything, Pepper is designed to keep people company.

its own words and actions to fit the situation. The robot can access a database to answer questions. It updates the database with its own answers and reactions. Pepper can also sing, dance, and tell jokes.

Besides working as a store greeter, Pepper could potentially be a helper for the elderly or for teachers. On June 20, 2015, Pepper went on sale in Japan. The supply of robots quickly sold out.

1,000
Number of Pepper robots that went on sale in June 2015.

- Social robots attempt to act like and understand humans.
- Pepper is a robot built to interact with humans.
- It understands human expressions and body language.
- Pepper greets customers for a Japanese company.
- Designers hope Pepper and robots like it can help the elderly and teachers.

Fact Sheet

- The largest swarm of robots was recently put together at Harvard University. The tiny Kilobot is about the size of a quarter, with three pin-like legs. Each robot is programmed with simple rules for motion. The researcher can send a signal to the swarm to have it form a certain shape, such as a starfish. The Kilobots then move slowly into the shape.

- Many roboticists are working to make robots work better with humans. First of all, robots need to be able to operate without accidently harming people. Industrial robots have been working in factories since the early 1960s. But those robots are usually working away from humans. They are not made to sense nearby humans and would not be able to react if someone got too close. Today, industrial robots are being programmed with more awareness. Baxter is an industrial robot that can be programmed for many tasks. It can also sense people working nearby. Baxter slows down what it's doing to avoid hurting people. And its fellow workers can tell whether Baxter has seen them through its facial and body cues.

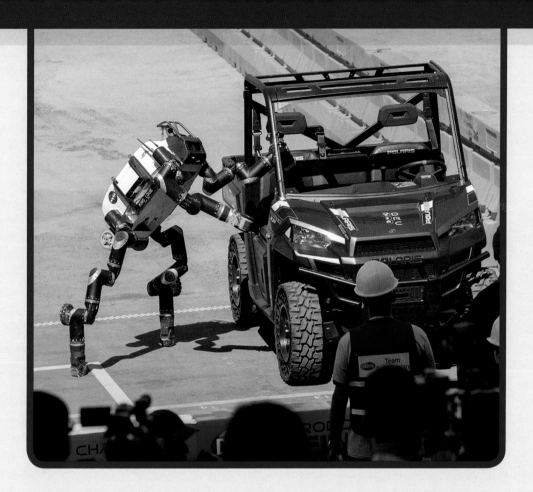

- A number of robots are being developed to investigate safe human-robotic interaction. For instance, the Italian Institute of Technology designed a robot that looks like a human toddler. iCub can interact with people, respond to voice commands, and learn to recognize new objects. iCub is an open-source robotics platform. This means it can be shared with other researchers to help make it better.

- Another open-source social robot is NAO. It's a small, programmable, humanoid robot. Much like Pepper, NAO is designed to recognize and respond to humans. The robot is already used in education. Schools in more than 70 countries use NAO in computer and science classes.

Glossary

alloy
A metal made from other metals.

bionic
Artificial body parts that work with natural ones.

exoskeleton
A supportive or protective structure on the outside of the body.

gesture
A movement used to express an idea.

gravity
The force that moves objects toward each other.

humanoid
Having human form or characteristics.

industrial
Used in factories.

joystick
A lever that can be moved in several directions to control something's movement.

modular
Constructed in similar sizes or with similar units for flexibility and variety of use.

neutron
A small particle with no electrical charge.

sensor
A device that detects a physical quality and responds by sending a signal.

For More Information

Books

Ceceri, Kathy. *Making Simple Robots: Exploring Cutting-Edge Robotics with Everyday Stuff*. San Francisco, CA: Maker Media, 2015.

Murphy, Maggie. *High-Tech DIY Projects with Robotics*. New York: Powerkids, 2015.

O'Hearn, Michael. *Awesome Space Robots*. Mankato, MN: Capstone, 2013.

Stewart, Melissa. *National Geographic Readers: Robots*. Washington, DC: National Geographic, 2014.

Visit 12StoryLibrary.com

Scan the code or use your school's login at **12StoryLibrary.com** for recent updates about this topic and a full digital version of this book. Enjoy free access to:

- Digital ebook
- Breaking news updates
- Live content feeds
- Videos, interactive maps, and graphics
- Additional web resources

Note to educators: Visit 12StoryLibrary.com/register to sign up for free premium website access. Enjoy live content plus a full digital version of every 12-Story Library book you own for every student at your school.

Index

About the Author

Angie Smibert is the author of several science fiction novels, numerous short stories, and many nonfiction titles. She was also a writer at NASA's Kennedy Space Center for many years. She has received NASA's Silver Snoopy award as well as several other awards for her work.